1. What does this booklet offer?

In the current educational climate, there is no shortage of encouragement – and pressure – for teachers to work more effectively in order to improve students' grades. Nor is there any shortage of advice about how this might be done. Teachers face a constant stream of initiatives and guidelines that purport to help them raise educational standards. All too often, the enthusiasm of their proponents is not matched by evidence that they will be either feasible or effective in practice.

Like many other publications, this booklet offers advice to teachers on how to interact more effectively with learners, and to encourage more student-to-student interaction, thereby promoting students' learning in the modern foreign languages (MFL) classroom. Also in line with many existing publications, it seeks to make explicit and build on what effective language teachers already do. The difference is that that the advice given here is backed up by rigorous evidence – summarised in section 2 – that it is likely to be effective, and that it is feasible in real classrooms.

There are important differences between MFL and other school subjects, and some of these are explored in section 3, and

in s[...] that tea[...] focu[...] implementing formative assessment in the MFL classroom, and the final section outlines how formative assessment can be developed within an MFL department.

2. Background

Beginning with the work of Gary Natriello and Terry Crooks in the late 1980s (Natriello 1987; Crooks 1988), the past 20 years have seen a steady accumulation of evidence that formative assessment is one of the most powerful ways to increase student engagement and achievement. In 1998, Black and Wiliam updated the reviews of Natriello and Crooks (Black and Wiliam 1998a) and also began to draw out some of the policy implications of this work in a booklet entitled *Inside the Black Box* (Black and Wiliam 1998b). In the ten years since then, the Formative Assessment Research Group at King's College London has worked with many local authorities to explore how these findings could be implemented in real classrooms. The first implementation studies involved mathematics, science, and English teachers in Oxfordshire and Medway, and found that nearly all the teachers involved were positive about the effects that the project had for them (Black *et al.* 2003), and about the significant gains in test performance for the classes involved (Wiliam *et al.* 2004). The work in Oxfordshire and Medway was summarized in the second booklet in the Black Box Assessment for Learning series entitled *Working Inside the Black Box* (Black *et al.* 2002).

Following that initial project and the response to it by practitioners, members of the King's College London team have made literally hundreds of contributions to teachers' conferences and to school-based professional development sessions. They have also helped in developments on a larger scale, notably with the Scottish Educational Education Department and with the States of Jersey. This led to the King's College team's direct contribution to the development of formative assessment as a significant component of the DfES Secondary Strategy (DfES 2004).

We have also worked specifically with groups of teachers of MFL (principally in Hampshire) and have found that the principles of formative assessment work as well in MFL classrooms as they do in mathematics, science and English classrooms.

From this work, and in particular by working with whole-school assessment teams, we have gained a greater understanding of the *generic* features of formative assessment (i.e. those that apply to learning across all stages and all school subjects), and also of those that are *specific* to particular phases (e.g., infant classes) and to individual subjects in the secondary school. The focus in this booklet is on the needs and opportunities relevant to secondary MFL teachers, although many of the ideas can be transferred and are adaptable for the primary classroom as examples are drawn from both secondary and primary classrooms.

3. The context of MFL Teaching

The study of MFL occupies a unique place in the curriculum. As English has become the global *lingua franca*, the argument that students need to study languages in order to be able to communicate effectively to others around the world rings increasingly hollow. However, as Harris (Harris and Nelson 1992) has remarked, bilingualism is the rule rather than the exception in many, if not most, parts of the world, and the Common European Framework (Council of Europe 2001) promotes the need for multilingual capability. For those who do not speak English, English is of course an obvious choice for a second language, but for native English speakers, the choice is not so clear; Spanish, Mandarin, and Arabic are spoken by hundreds of millions, although most of our schools are much better equipped to teach French, German and Spanish. By learning another language, students can acquire new ways of looking at the world, and also can gain insights into their own language (it is often argued that one never really understands grammar until one learns a second language). This has been recognised by the government's decision that all primary school students at Key Stage 2 should be given the opportunity to learn a language and its reconsideration of language-learning pathways for the 14–19 age group.

In England, the National Curriculum provides a framework of attainment targets and level descriptions that determine what needs to be covered in the MFL curriculum. The most recent guidelines enable teachers to plan lessons and schemes of work and to wrap these objectives around the desired language content in a meaningful way. Cross-phase planning increasingly takes into consideration the new 7–14 continuum of learning (Jones 2005), providing a pathway for students to progress from their primary MFL learning experiences to the secondary phase. The Key Stage 2 *Framework for Languages*, the Key Stage 3 *Framework for Teaching MFL* and the National Curriculum have

overlapping strands that align with the literacy initiative and build upon primary students' familiarity with target-setting. It is therefore much easier than it was to develop learning trajectories in MFL that are coherent, structured, progressive and differentiated (thus also consistent with the agenda of personalised learning). Such coherence meshes well with a formative approach where language learning is demystified by sharing with the students learning intentions and success criteria. This is crucial, given the findings of research with Year 9 students which showed that, although the majority of students were positive about their language learning:

These pupils lack a clear view of what learning a language really means. They are unclear about what they are supposed to be gaining from their lessons. (Lee *et al.* 1998, p. 5)

Well-thought-out learning objectives can enable students to make progress in their learning of a foreign language, and to develop the capacity to own and monitor their own progress as independent language users – the ultimate aim of language learning. In classroom-based learning, students also need to be conversant with ways of talking about language (sometimes called meta-language) so that they can utilise the greatest possible range of strategies in their lifelong language learning endeavours. Becoming familiar with the language of assessment will furthermore ensure that students can derive the utmost benefit from the formative approach. Where this language is interpreted in the target language, further opportunities for authentic target language use arise, making the language learning classroom multilingual in more ways than one.

Information and communication technology (ICT) is used increasingly in MFL teaching and learning and provides valuable opportunities for learning that is self-directed, but still interactive. These are key factors in a formative approach both in the MFL classroom and beyond, allowing students to direct their learning independently both within school and in society.

Formative assessment fits naturally into the MFL learning setting, since teachers can collect and sift data that arises in classroom interactions and activities, so that professional judgements can be made about the next steps in learning. In a classroom culture that values and rewards participation, rather than penalising mistakes, students will feel encouraged to 'have a go', thus signalling to the teacher their current level of understanding, providing more reliable feedback to the teacher and an additional opportunity for authentic language use.

A formative approach requires a further critical reappraisal of the use of English, which may then have a clearer role in supporting target language learning (Cooke 2001). While we believe that formative assessment is consistent with the goals of MFL teaching, certain assumptions about the use of the target language that preclude the development of formative assessment in MFL classrooms may need to be moderated. The judicious use of English provides an opportunity for students to become more active learners, to use their knowledge about language to help them in learning a foreign language and to reap the benefits of formative assessment. We should make it clear, however, that we do not in any way advocate a return to lessons that take place in a 'gale of English'. In our view, the majority of MFL teaching should be in the target language, thereby maximising exposure to the target language and providing opportunities to think about using it creatively, and validating it as a legitimate medium of communication and instruction.

This booklet highlights some particular features of the MFL learning experience that readily interface with formative assessment approaches based on key principles of learning that are part of an effective classroom community of MFL learning.

4. Principles of learning

Of all the various opportunities for feedback in classrooms, two types are essential to formative assessment: the first is from student to teacher, the second from teacher to student. Learning is supported by alternation between these, in which each contribution responds to the other. The MFL classroom presents a unique situation in that the interaction between student and teacher is conducted to a great extent in the foreign language as communication on a meta-level. Learning in this particular environment can be facilitated when teaching is based on four principles of learning.

The **first** of these principles within this conceptual framework consists in meeting the students at their level of knowledge, i.e. revisiting prior learning in the form of revision. This allows the teacher to verify that the student has understood what has previously been learnt as well as clarifying any outstanding questions, thus providing a basis for the introduction of new material. The structures can then be extended and consolidated using the four skills of listening, speaking, reading and writing. During this process the teacher listens to responses, provides feedback and sets challenges to actively involve the students, implementing a **second** principle of learning, which is that students must be active in the process – learning has to be done *by* them, it cannot be done *for* them.

The **third** principle is crucial for the learning process as the teacher needs to introduce the learning objectives and the students learn to understand these as a frame of reference for the evaluation and improvement of their own work. In short, the learners have to establish *what* they are working towards, *where* they stand in relation to the criteria of what is considered quality work and discover ways and ask questions aimed at clarifying *how* to get there. Successful learners become aware that the process is not linear but a spiral of refinement and amendment. They thus learn to evaluate their work from a more detached point of view. The students need, and this is the **fourth** principle, to talk about their work using language learning activities based on peer and self-assessment. The students receive feedback from both teachers and other learners in the class and can develop critical judgement, allowing them to improve the quality of their work. When students are able to engage meaningfully with the learning objectives and their criteria, they begin to take ownership of their learning.

5. Questioning, questions and dialogue in the MFL classroom

Good language teaching has always been underpinned by effective questioning techniques. The starting point for many classroom dialogues is the familiar initiation–response–feedback (IRF) format, which was elaborated by Sinclair and Coulthard (1975) in their study of classroom discourse. A typical IRF is as follows, where the teacher is practising animal vocabulary with flashcards (a cat in this case):

T: *Was ist das?*
S: *Es ist eine Katze.*
T: *Ja, das ist eine Katze, das ist korrekt.*

Teachers often use the IRF sequence to facilitate student responses in the early stages of pattern practice where predictable answers are required, e.g., to establish a vocabulary subset. This also enables the teacher at this stage to establish good pronunciation habits and to reinforce the gender of nouns and adjectives. It is, however, important to move beyond these ritualised and rather limiting classroom interactions as soon as possible for the following reasons.

The first is that in most classrooms, after the teacher has asked a question, it is the students who decide whether to participate by raising their hands. In such a classroom some students are participating, volunteering to answer every question, while others are attempting to avoid the teacher's gaze, so as not to get called upon. The reason this is so serious is because recent research has shown that the intelligence of students is actually increased by participating in active discussion, but that students tend to choose for themselves environments that match their preferred level of cognitive functioning (Dickens and Flynn, 2001; Mercer *et al.* 2004). The students who actively participate in such classroom interactions are actually increasing their cognitive abilities, while those who are seeking to avoid participation are foregoing that opportunity. Allowing students to decide whether to participate or not therefore increases the achievement gap between the lowest- and highest-achieving students. Clearly it is crucial that teachers provide strategies to enable students to participate at their level when they may be lacking in confidence.

For this reason, many teachers have adopted a classroom rule of 'No hands up except to *ask* a question'. Students are allowed to raise their hands in order to ask the teacher a question, but if the teacher has asked a question, it is the teacher who chooses who to call upon for an answer. Of course, there are some occasions when such a rule is unhelpful, for example, if the teacher wants to know whether any members of the class have a different answer to one given by a particular student. For that reason, one MFL teacher created a big cardboard arm, with a pointing finger, with a drawing pin through the middle. When the finger was pointing upwards, students could raise their hands to signal that they wanted to make a contribution, but when it was pointing down (as it was for the majority of the time), it was the teacher who chose who to answer. One primary teacher uses a puppet for the same purpose.

The use of 'No hands up except to ask a question' increases student engagement dramatically, and can be used with a wide variety of questions. For example, one teacher in a school in the London Borough of Redbridge regularly spells out a French word using the French alphabet: S-T-Y-L-O and then chooses a student at random to say what the word spelled out is in English. Many teachers are surprised how difficult it is to choose students at random, because a desire to keep the pace of the lesson going seems to lead them to choose, subconsciously, students who are likely to give the correct response. For this reason, teachers have found it useful to write the names of all students on lollipop sticks or small cards, in order to choose students truly at random (it is, of course, essential to replace the names when they are drawn, for otherwise the chosen student will know he or she is off the hook for the next 29 or so questions).

Such a change in the classroom climate is, of course, something of a shock to many students, so many teachers have softened the impact somewhat by, for example, allowing students selected to answer a question to 'phone a friend', or, where the question is in multiple-choice format, to 'ask the audience' or go '50-50' (where half of the response options are removed).

Sometimes, students will respond by saying that they do not know. This may be because they genuinely do not know, in which case, the teacher might say, 'OK, I'll come back to you' and proceed to collect responses from other members of the class, after which the teacher returns to the student originally selected and asks, 'Which of these answers do you like best?' The important thing about such an exchange is that the students' response of 'I don't know' does not get them off the hook – they have to listen to the subsequent discussion because they know the teacher will return to them. Occasionally, a student's response of 'I don't know' may be caused not by a lack of knowledge, but by an unwillingness to engage. In such situations, many teachers have found that saying; 'Yes, but if you did know, what would you say?' produces remarkably sensible responses from students. The common feature in all these responses is that even if the student resists engaging in the discussion, the teacher keeps a clear focus on insisting that all students are required to participate.

The second limitation of the standard IRF format is that the rapid-fire questioning, even when students are chosen at random, can quickly deteriorate into a formulaic repetition of well-rehearsed routines. Such exchanges can look very impressive, and for this reason are frequently held up as examples of 'pace' in lessons in official videos, but such rapid-fire exchanges have little or nothing to do with learning. They do speed up recall of familiar vocabulary, but these effects atrophy quite quickly, and the amount of new learning that takes place during such exchanges is negligible, because thought is impossible at such speed. True pace in lessons comes from ensuring that as much of the available time as possible is spent on activities that generate meaningful and lasting learning, which means building in more time for thinking, and spending less time merely reacting. As Jones and Swarbrick (2004) argue, 'If we do not offer cognitive challenge, if we do not demand thought from students, then they are unlikely to take MFL seriously' (p. 65). Indeed, as McPake *et al.* (1999) found, one of the most significant criticisms that upper secondary school students in Scotland had of their MFL lessons was that the lessons did not make them think enough.

The third limitation of the standard IRF format is that, too often, the intellectual 'heavy lifting' is done almost entirely by the teacher. Even when the teacher chooses students at random, and allows them time to respond, the classroom exchanges are a series of one-to-one exchanges – what might be described as 'serial table-tennis'. In order to allow the classroom discourse to build on the contributions of students, teachers have explored a variety of different techniques. For example, in 'question basketball', the teacher asks a question of one student, chosen at random, of course, then chooses a second at random for an evaluation of the answer, and perhaps a third, again at random, to provide an explanation of why the answer is correct or incorrect. Such classroom dialogue is much more demanding of the teacher, since he or she needs to listen carefully to student responses, looking for opportunities for divergence, expansion and creativity in both question and answer. However, in the most effective such classrooms, the teacher becomes more like a conductor than a featured soloist, bringing the voices of different students into the discussion, and developing much greater student autonomy.

Rich questions

Although most teachers are aware of the distinction between open and closed questions, this turns out to be much less important than whether the question is of low order, requiring only recall or application of a simple rule, or high order, requiring thought. For example, *Is the verb 'être' regular?* is a low-order question for most students. You either know it or you don't. However, the question, *What does it mean for a verb to be irregular?* is a high-order question, requiring students to think in order to answer. And there not much point in knowing the answer to the first question if you can't answer the second.

In practice, the distinction between closed and open questions, and between low-order and higher-order questions is not quite as clear-cut as it might seem. For example, the question about the regularity of the verb *être* mentioned above might be a higher-order question for some students; if they do not know the answer by rote, but can conjugate the present tense of *être* from memory, they might use their knowledge of the conjugation of regular verbs in French to discover that *être* does not follow the regular patterns, and so is irregular. And although this question seems like a very closed question, it can be opened up by asking students whether the fact that a verb is irregular in the present tense necessarily means it is irregular in the past, or the future

tense. Although some teachers can do this 'on-the-fly', for most teachers it is careful planning of a range of possible questions that makes successful classroom dialogue.

Consider the following case of a Year 8 German class learning the key vocabulary of transport – going by bus, train, bike, etc. – using a classic three-stage questioning routine. The teacher started with basic factual naming questions, and moved on to more open-ended ones (and back again), and used a variety of techniques (including flashcards, actions and games) to consolidate the learning. One student wanted to say he went to school on his skateboard and having learnt the structure in German that involves the dative e.g. as in *Ich fahre **mit** dem Auto*, speculated understandably that the same rule would apply for a skateboard. This in fact is not the case with a skateboard – the name in German is also *Skateboard* but the rule is not the same – *Ich fahre Skateboard* and the teacher gave the student the task of finding out how to say it correctly.

The teacher then moved in subsequent lessons to a more imaginative travel scenario involving travelling to the moon. The students were asked to think of creative solutions for travelling there and had to utilise previously learnt vocabulary, such as size, colours and numbers of windows, to describe the type of spacecraft being used, in both oral presentations and in written descriptions. Students who need to become proficient in asking as well as responding to questions, were well rehearsed in basic question formats by the teacher (*How many passengers can the craft take?*, *How big is it?*) so that they could ask different questions of each other. This was extended to the use of a more speculative type of question from the teacher, using, for example, the conditional tense (*Would it need a pilot?*, *How much would it cost?*) and the future tense (*Will it go directly to the moon or stop on the way?*). The students responded appropriately, with careful scaffolding by the teacher. The whole sequence provided an opportunity for combining new with known language items, allowing the teacher to evaluate the quality of previous learning.

Sometimes questions can be used to encourage learners to reflect both on what they think and what they have heard from others, which is an essential stage in developing understanding. Developing extended or alternative answers might involve the teacher probing in the following way, using the target language:

What can we add to Yagnesh's answer?
(In this case, the teacher could provide a series of alternatives.)

Do you agree with Suzie's answer?
(Here the teacher could take a show of hands on who agreed or disagreed and students could be asked, in pairs, to provide a reason.)

Can someone improve on Jack's answer?
(A suitable prompt might be for the teacher to suggest using a connective for a richer description.)

Teachers need to be patient and wait for the various ideas to be revealed before they start correcting and directing the responses, providing scaffolding as necessary but allowing students time to develop their answers (perhaps by encouraging them to try out answers with partner before being asked to share with the whole class). Most teachers find allowing adequate 'wait time' difficult at first, but Black *et al.* (2003) found that when teachers did allow more time for students to develop, and to elaborate, their answers, then:

- longer answers were given than previously;
- more students were choosing to answer;
- fewer students refused to answer;
- students commented on or added to the answers of other students;
- more alternative explanations or examples were offered.

Above all, teachers need to plan for increasingly more linguistically challenging questions which, even as lower-order questions, cannot be answered just with 'reproduced' language.

All-student response systems

Selecting students to answer questions at random increases the level of engagement in the whole class, and also broadens the information the teacher has about the class's progress. Instead of hearing only from those who think they know the answer (surely a biased sample), the teacher gets information from a randomly chosen student, which is likely to be more representative. However, the teacher is still only getting information from a small number of students, and as such, this information is of limited usefulness in deciding whether the class has sufficient understanding to allow the teacher to move on.

In order to broaden the information base, many teachers have made systematic use of 'all-student response systems' in which every student is expected to respond simultaneously. At its simplest, this requires no equipment at all. The teacher might point to a word (e.g., a past participle of a verb) in a piece of text on the board or interactive white-board and ask the class *Is this word correct?* Rather than calling on an individual to respond, the teacher can ask the whole class to respond, with a 'thumbs up' if the word is spelled correctly, and with a 'thumbs

down' if it is not. This technique has two clear benefits. The first is that every student is under pressure to 'vote' on the question, since it is immediately apparent if a student has not expressed a view. The second is that the teacher has a good grasp of the level of understanding in the class. If everyone answers correctly, the teacher can move on. If no one answers correctly, then the teacher might go over the point again. But if some of the class have answered correctly, and some have not, then this creates a 'teachable moment'. The teacher can turn to one student and say, 'You thought it was correct. Why?' and then turn to another and say, 'You thought it was incorrect. Why?' Because the teacher knows, from the initial voting, who has answered correctly and who has not, she is able to orchestrate a much more effective discussion.

Where there are a number of possible responses, there are a number of possibilities. Where the variety of responses is predictable, the teacher can use class-sets of cards with the letters A, B, C, D, E, etc., or just ask students to hold up the appropriate number of fingers for the correct response (A = 1, B = 2, C = 3, . . .). Where the variety of responses is not predictable, teachers can use dry-erase boards that students can use to indicate their answers. For example, a Spanish teacher used the following item during a lesson on the indirect object pronoun and its correct placement:

Which of the following is the correct translation of 'I give the book to him'?

A. *Yo lo doy el libro.*

B. *Yo doy le el libro.*

C. *Yo le doy el libro.*

D. *Yo doy lo el libro.*

E. *Yo doy el libro le.*

F. *Yo doy el libro lo.*

This item is diagnostic because it has been designed so that if students answer incorrectly, it is easy to work out why. Response A indicates a pronoun error, responses B and E indicate placement errors, and responses D and F indicate both pronoun and placement errors. Through careful planning of questions before the lesson, teachers can check, in a very meaningful and deep way, the understanding of every student in the class in 'real time' and make adjustments to their teaching while the students are still in front of them, rather than waiting until their books are marked.

Some teachers worry that students will look at the responses of others before giving their own. One teacher's response to this was to make students put their heads down on their desks and hold their hands in the air. Other teachers make a point of picking on students who changed their vote and ask them 'Why did you change your vote?' However, most teachers find that after a few days, students stop worrying about other people's answers and concentrate on their own. In fact, many students have said they prefer these 'all-student response systems'. One girl said, 'If the teacher picks on you and you get it wrong, you think you're the only one who didn't get it, but with the [ABCDE] cards, there's always someone else who got the same answer as you, so you don't feel so on your own.'

Some teachers have used these diagnostic questions with classroom 'clickers' – wireless devices that students can use to signal their response to a multiple-choice question, which are collected by a receiver and sent to the teacher's computer for analysis, for example, as a bar chart displaying how many students chose each option. This has two advantages: the students' responses are anonymous and the system keeps a record of the students' responses. However, the technology available currently has one major drawback, and that is that it can be used only with questions where there is a single correct response. As such, there is a real possibility that some students will get the correct answer by guessing. Where there are multiple correct responses, or where the answer has to be constructed by the student, provided the question is well designed, it is highly unlikely that a student would get the correct answer for the wrong reason.

With adaptation, almost all the activities that MFL teachers already use for single-student responses can be adapted for use as an all-student response activity. To take another example, a teacher could use an overhead projector or an interactive whiteboard (or, indeed, a chalkboard) to present to the class a paragraph of text in the target language. Five points in the text (some of which are errors and some not) are labelled with A, B, C, D and E, and the students have to use ABCDE cards to indicate where they think the errors are.

6. Feedback

The only effective feedback is that which is used. This may seem blindingly obvious, but in practice most of the feedback that MFL teachers give their students is not used by their students, and serves only to show how diligent the teacher has been in marking the students' work. This is because most of the feedback that students get is what psychologists call 'ego-involving', focusing on the value of the student as a good or bad achiever,

emphasising overall judgement by marks, grades, rank-order lists, and so on. The effect of this kind of feedback is negative for all students. It discourages the low attainers, and makes high attainers avoid tasks if they cannot see their way to success, for failure would be seen as bad news about themselves rather than as an opportunity to learn. It also encourages cheating, because what matters is the mark or grade, not the learning it denotes. In contrast, where feedback is 'task involving', the focus of the feedback is not on the person but on the strengths and weaknesses of the particular student output, emphasising what needs to be done to improve, and ideally, how to go about it. Put simply, to be effective, feedback must cause the students to engage in some form of thinking, rather than an emotional reaction based on whether they did better or worse than their neighbour.

Many teachers realise that grades or marks are not helpful, but because of school assessment policies, they try to compromise by giving students both marks and comments, hoping to get the 'best of both worlds'. However, as research by Butler (1987), Dweck (2000) and others has shown, giving students marks and comments has the same effect as giving just marks: the high achieving students don't need to read the comments, and the low-achieving students don't want to.

All that has happened is that the teacher has wasted a lot of time giving feedback that will have no impact on student learning. Indeed, as Butler pointed out, when students were given both marks and comments, the first thing they looked at was, predictably, the mark, but the second thing they looked at was their neighbour's mark (Butler 1987).

General responses in the form of exclamations such as *Sehr gut!*, *Super!* and so on have their place as instant feedback, particularly when spoken tasks are involved, but the research suggests that they are completely irrelevant for formal marking. What is needed is feedback that looks forward to the next steps in learning, not backwards at what has and has not been learned. And yet very few teachers believe that their students spend as long taking on board feedback as it takes the teacher to provide it, which is probably why teachers tend to be more tired than their students at the end of the day – the wrong people are doing all the work! In short, most teachers give students far too much feedback, but of the wrong sort, and do not make the students accountable for actually using the feedback to improve.

One simple technique to force students to engage with feedback is to tell them how many errors there are, but not what they are. For example, if the student has completed an exercise with ten questions each requiring a single word answer (e.g., a drill on past participles), the student would be told only that three of the ten were wrong, and it is her or his task to 'find them and fix them'. Similarly, when marking a final draft of a piece of writing in the target language, rather than correct every error, the teacher can put a dot in the margin each time there is an error in the line. For weaker students, rather than a dot, the teacher can put a 'g' for an error in grammar, an 's' for a spelling mistake, and so on, thus providing a degree of personalisation in the feedback. This can be combined with more general comments, as in the following example:

A well-planned piece of work with lots of detail. Well done for using the vocabulary we learnt in class. Now use the textbook, page 20, to help you correct your spelling mistakes. There are about five, but possibly more!

Another technique that forces the student to engage with the feedback is to mark the location of every error in a final draft, and to return it to the student with instructions to classify the error (e.g., adjective–noun agreement, pronoun errors, placement errors, etc.). Students can then keep a 'tally' of the errors they are making, decide on priorities for improvement, and, by consulting peers who have complementary difficulties, help each other.

As noted above, comments should focus on what needs to be done to improve the work, rather than what's wrong with it now. Feedback that merely points out weaknesses is likely to be no more useful than the advice once given to a bad comedian: *Be funnier*. Compare these two comments on a student's work designing posters with information in the target language about recycling:

1. *A nice picture but you need to add more writing.*
2. *Your poster catches my eye but I am wondering why I should really want to recycle my rubbish! Can you persuade me? How about some imperatives? Some statistics that might encourage me to take action! What can I do? What should I do?*

The first comment points out the shortcomings of the piece. In contrast to this, the second comment initiates thinking immediately, enabling the learner to discuss her thoughts either with the teacher or another student, while the questioning nature encourages the student to initiate improvement. Many teachers find generating such comments difficult to start with, but this is often because the aims of the activity were not clear in the first place. When the teacher has provided the students with learning intentions or success criteria, it is much easier to 'close the loop', focusing the comments on the desired learning.

Of course, as noted above, the feedback is useful only if it is used, and checking whether students have, in fact, acted on the comments provided can be difficult, so some teachers write their comments on a separate sheet. When the student has responded to the comment, the student puts the sheet inside her or his exercise book at the page where they have addressed the comment.

When the teacher takes the book in for marking, he or she can use this as a reminder of the feedback given, and then check on the student's response, without having to leaf through all the pages.

Another effective way of giving feedback is to set targets for the students. In doing so, it is important to be clear about whether the targets relate to the current work, or are for students to take forward in other work. In general, when the targets relate to current work, they should be focused and specific, but where the feedback is intended to improve future work, they need to be more general.

In order to promote deep learning, it is not enough just to get the students to 'react' to the feedback. The feedback should encourage reflection. For example, if a student has been asked to write a description of a male pop star, here are two possible responses:

1. *Now do a description of a female.*
2. *If you were to write this description again but changing the subject to a female, what changes would you have to make?*

Whereas the first comment gives the student a task to perform to improve his or her work output, the second comment initiates thinking and reflecting immediately about the original work, thus following up on the task and pushing the student to tackle the problematic issue of gender. Such feedback also then leads naturally on to peer-assessment activities (see below).

Sometimes, directing students where to go for help and what to do to improve can be effective, as in the following examples:

You have understood perfectly how to use 'um' and 'zu' clauses. Look out for your past participles after you've used an auxiliary verb. Look back in the notes we made for how to translate 'for' in different situations and rewrite the phrases.

With the use of such constructive feedback, teachers engage in an ongoing dialogue with students, concentrating on *how* to improve their work and *how* to take the learning forward, also made explicit in the following comment:

Good description of your favourite programmes. You use effective long sentences and your use of accents is perfect. Next time try and use the past tense or the future tense in your work to be able to reach a level 5.

Comments like these take a teacher quite some time to write – our experience is that marking in this way takes about twice as long as 'traditional' marking – so it needs to be used sparingly. Our recommendation would be that teachers should not attempt to write extended comments on more than a quarter of the work that students produce. For the other three-quarters, self-assessment, peer-assessment, 'find them and fix them' feedback and other quick checks by the teacher should be the norm. As the students become increasingly proficient in the language, it becomes possible to give some feedback in the target language, a useful differentiated challenge in itself for high attainers. For further discussion of planning for assessment in MFL, see Barnes and Hunt (2003).

7. Activating students as learning resources for one another

The previous two sections – on questioning and feedback – have focused on the teacher's role in keeping learning 'on track'. However, as many teachers never tire of telling their students, 'there is more than one teacher in this room' and students have a vital role to play in taking responsibility for their own learning, and in supporting the learning of their peers, which is the focus of this section. Some teachers are reluctant to make time for students to help each other, believing it to be either inefficient, or an abdication of the teacher's responsibilities. Students too come to believe that if they are asked to help others in the class, they are being slowed down in their learning, and the constant pressure on teachers to differentiate and personalise learning exacerbates this.

In fact, there have been many studies that show that when students help each other, it is those who *give* help that benefit most, because the demands of explaining something to someone else forces one to deepen one's thinking. This is something that all teachers realise intuitively when they say, 'I never understood this until I had to teach it.' When students help each other, this does provide differentiation, but in depth rather than breadth. The higher-achieving students may not be ready for GCSE when they are 14, but their understanding will be greatly deepened by their experiences of supporting their peers, and they are less likely to forget what they have learned.

Effective collaborative learning can take many forms. Many teachers are well used to getting students working with 'buzz' partners; they first discuss their responses to a question in pairs or groups before sharing them with the whole class. This provides an opportunity for students to develop and rehearse their answers, and to be more reflective.

A slightly more structured approach to the same principle was used in a Year 10 German lesson. The teacher asked the students to move to one side of the classroom or the other depending on whether they liked a well-known fast food outlet. She then asked them to form smaller groups and to put together their reasons, in writing. A representative of each group then gave a verbal report, in German, in which taste, value for money, and health concerns were common threads. An important feature of this exchange was that the students were actively encouraged to give it their best try, however imperfect, and to switch back to English to get support from their group when necessary.

In another classroom, a teacher was working on developing a good accent for spoken French. Each students was given a paragraph of French text, and the class was divided into six groups. Within each group, each student read the paragraph to the rest of the group and then the group voted on who had the best French accent to represent the group. In the subsequent whole-class session, the six representatives read out the paragraph, and the class voted on the best accent, followed by a whole-class discussion of what made a good French accent. A Year 10 teacher used a similar approach, asking a Year 10 class to work in small groups to create dialogues on a given topic to be performed to the whole class. Following discussion with students about what they would be looking for in terms of pronunciation of key words (such as silent endings), agreements and liaison, for example, on the basis of these criteria, students assessed each other's contributions, consolidating learning on a collective basis by hearing correct or incorrect pronunciation.

Where students are giving written feedback on each other's work, many teachers have been concerned about what students will write about their peer's efforts. If there is concern on this point, the teacher can begin by giving the students Post-it® notes on which to write feedback to their peers. However, most teachers find that the students' comments on each other's work are so sensible (and often much harder hitting than the teacher would dare to write) that it is possible to dispense with the Post-it® notes after a few weeks (or even days).

It is also helpful to provide students with a structure for the peer-assessment, such as 'two stars and a wish' in which students have to say two positive things about the work on which they are commenting (the 'stars') and a wish for the work to be improved, as in the following example:

- *You have used a wide range of vocabulary.*
- *You give a vivid description of your weekend.*
- *You need to be careful not to mix up the auxiliary verbs ('avoir' and 'être') when writing about the past. Write three further sentences in the past using the avoir auxiliary and three sentences using 'être'. You can use the notes on the passé composé in your grammar book to help you.*

Even young children can learn how to focus in this way and, by giving positive feedback to other students in their class, help to create a classroom culture of support for their own learning (see Jones and Coffey 2006, Chapter 7 on Assessment). Some Year 5 children were working in threes, one being assessed, one asking questions and one assessing, using a 'two stars and a wish' proforma created by the teacher. The key question was: *Was machst du am (Montag, Dienstag,* etc.)? The children replied by choosing one of seven pictures (of swimming, dancing, playing football, playing tennis, shopping, cycling, staying at home) and placing a counter on the relevant picture, choosing from *Ich gehe schwimmen / tanzen / Fussball spielen / Tennis spielen / einkaufen / Fahrrad fahren / bleibe zu Hause. Ich gehe gern / nicht gern schwimmen* etc. Here are some samples of the children's feedback to each other:

Luke to Liam: *You are very good at saying what you do. You can say if you don't like something. You need to work on 'Fussball spielen'.*

Thomas to Jade: *You know your days of the week. You know your activities. A wish . . . to say if you like it or not.*

James to Mona: *You can say what you're doing. You can say 'Ich gehe' very well. You need to work on what you like or don't like doing.*

Another example of peer assessment involved Year 7 students looking at letters that had been drafted for homework in French and which were evaluated as a class activity. The teacher began by drawing up a set of success criteria in discussion with the students. Students then worked in pairs discussing their two letters and noted ideas from each other, and suggestions from the teacher about improvements such as the use of connectives, better qualifiers, or greater use of past or future tenses. They also had to give an overall evaluation about the effectiveness of the letter in terms of general readability. This task made for a very good use of learning time and validated the homework immediately.

The students reported that they were nervous at first about assessing their friends' work but once they had confidence, they did it with great care and sensitivity and learned from each other. Students can gradually acquire habits and skills of collaborative learning from an early age, and, through peer-assessment, develop the objectivity required for self-assessment.

As with other formative assessment techniques, students will need support and practice in assessing the work of other learners, and it is generally a good idea to start with the most straightforward forms of peer-assessment. For example, students can swap books and check for specific items such as correct spellings, accents or gender and write a comment, possibly using the 'two stars and a wish' structure.

To begin with, it is often a good idea to provide the students with clear success criteria, such as the following list for a Year 7 unit on 'Introducing myself' in French:

- using an appropriate phrase to say one's name;
- writing age using the verb *avoir*;
- incorporating all the elements of a birth date – article, day, month;
- description of family members with appropriate articles and possessives;
- writing where one lives and in what type of dwelling.

A teacher observed undertaking this activity constructed an overhead projector transparecy (OHT) with the class putting together all these components. Together teacher and students identified correct linguistic models from the textbook that served as a source of reference. In pairs, the pieces of writing were swapped and students annotated each other's work. After some time, moving to a whole-class activity, the teacher drew the attention of the class to two pieces of writing on OHTs that the class discussed, evaluating the quality of each in terms of content and accuracy. They then wrote comments based on the agreed criteria on their partner's work using the 'two stars and a wish' structure, and discussed the points made with each other.

In a Spanish GCSE lesson, students had been given back pieces of extended writing about future plans and careers and were working in small groups. They looked at their own comments and read them out to each other. They then examined the pieces of work and identified the star points in each, then the wish elements and drew up criteria for a quality piece of writing on the topic. Groups eventually shared their ideas which were collated on a PC with data projector and which provided, with teacher support, a useful model of writing for future use and, crucially, for adaptation based on the criteria. With younger students, the criteria tend to be provided by the teacher and deduced by the students whereas with older students, they can work out the criteria inductively. In all cases, the process of composing/ drafting and the improving of the work in progress are as important as the final product.

Some teachers have also found it useful to help students improve the quality of their peer-assessments. They collect in the comments made by students during peer-assessment activities, and present them (anonymously) to the whole class, on either an OHP or an interactive whiteboard. By going through each comment, and discussing with the class whether the comment is helpful or not, teachers have found that the quality of comments made by peers improves rapidly.

The activities outlined here illustrate some techniques that many teachers have found useful in supporting effective peer-assessment and other forms of collaborative learning. As noted above, students who give help benefit in terms of a deeper understanding, and those who receive help benefit directly from that feedback. However, peer-assessment also plays an important role in developing *self*-assessment for all students. Many teachers report that students appear to find self-assessment extraordinarily difficult even when clear success criteria are provided. This is because, for many students, internalising the success criteria in the context of one's own work is just too emotionally charged (this is also why many students seem reluctant to check over their own work).

In peer-assessment, however, they have to internalise the success criteria in the context of someone else's work, which is much less emotionally charged. They learn to recognise both quality and inadequacies in other learners' work even if the level of work they are assessing is higher than the level at which they are operating consistently. They learn a meta-language that enables them to discuss their work with one another and provide feedback in a way that focuses on the task. Peer discussion enables each student to see the strengths and weaknesses of *their own* work with greater clarity, and to internalise the success criteria, which are then available to them in their own work. Such practice also helps students to see how small changes, additions or different ways of approaching parts of the work can raise the quality of the work. Peer-assessment therefore functions as a stepping-stone to self-assessment.

The growing availability of powerful ICT in classrooms creates the possibility of extending collaborative learning beyond the confines of the classroom. Individual or class blogs, online journals and electronic diaries allow students to take greater control of their learning. They can obtain, and respond to, feedback quickly, revisit their work, and enter into an extended dialogue capturing views and feedback from other students in the class, from other classes and even from other schools. Blogs and electronic diaries can be enriched with streamed videos and podcasts uploaded on the school's webspace, providing a natural forum for effective peer- and self-assessment. Finally, the increasing availability of video-conferencing enables students to have face-to-face conversations with native speakers and provides them with authentic opportunities to practise their skills. These meetings can be recorded or streamed on CDs or DVDs and played back to the students, allowing them to assess their learning.

8. Activating students as owners of their own learning

Supporting students in becoming owners of their own learning is an extraordinarily complex task. As well as requiring students to be able to think about their own thinking (which psychologists call metacognition), it involves establishing dispositions about the desirability of learning, and an ability to manage the emotional aspects of learning. The kinds of questioning that teachers use, ensuring that feedback promotes thinking rather than just the ranking of students, and the use of collaborative learning all have a role to play here. The systematic use of all these components creates a learning environment in which the focus of students is on personal growth rather than just protecting a sense of well-being. Within such an environment students resent being given work that is too easy, because they can see that engaging in that work will be a waste of time.

A teacher in a primary school in Scotland has a poster on her wall that reads: 'Stuck? Good. It was worth coming in today.' For this teacher, the only point of being in school is to be stuck, to be confused, provided the student has the resilience and the resourcefulness to act intelligently in such a situation. To become autonomous learners, students have to have a clear understanding of where they want to go in their learning, find ways of establishing where they are currently, and, most importantly, develop the determination and the capability to get there. Acquisition of these capabilities is challenging for the most mature learners, but their development can begin at an early age, as the following example shows.

A Year 6 class was learning about transport – the learning objective was to be able to use the German words for different means of transport (*mit dem Fahrrad, Roller, Traktor, Motorrad, Auto, Taxi, Bus,* *Zug, Hubschrauber, Flugzeug* and *zu Fuß*) in combination with both first and third person verbs (*Ich fahre/gehe; Er/Sie/Name fährt/geht*). The teacher provided toys, 3-D object handling being an important part of her MFL teaching.

The children worked in groups of three, with each group being given toys representing each mode of transport. One student asked the question: *Womit fährst du nach Hause?*, the second replied (e.g., *Ich fahre mit dem Zug. Tom/Bethany/Er/ Sie fährt mit dem Bus*) and the third was responsible for evaluating the response. The group used counters on a sheet of pictures to show which forms of transport were mentioned and to encourage use of all of them. To begin with, the children found it much easier to use the third person form with someone's name rather than the pronouns, but once the children were confident, *er/sie* were reintroduced, and the students recognised this as a learning challenge as the following self-assessments (following the 'two stars and a wish' format) show:

Rebecca
I am good at the modes of transport.
I have got good at using 'sie' and 'er'.
My wish, to pronounce my German r's.

Ben
I am good at using 'er' and 'sie' and remembering the order of words.

Good at remembering 'gehe zu Fuß'.
I need to remember the difference between 'Zug' and 'Flugzeug'.

Some teachers have used 'traffic light' icons to introduce and develop self-assessment skills, asking students to label their work green, amber or red according to whether they think they have good, partial or little understanding. Such a system provides information for the teacher about an individual student's confidence levels with structures and topics. If many students use red, the teacher can see clearly that this work has to be revisited. Conversely, a plethora of greens indicates that understanding (or at least the level of confidence) is good and the class is ready to move on whereas a mixture of reds, greens and ambers calls for different action. Traffic lighting is a simple technique that has added considerable value in the language classroom in that it allows the teacher to gauge comprehension. It can be used effectively in self- and peer-assessment, as in the following example, when peer-assessing role play work:

- green – better than I could have done, and I got ideas from this role play;
- amber – about the same quality as I could do;
- red – some bits of the role play seem to be missing or incorrect.

After all the presentations students explain their evaluations and thereby develop a shared understanding of what 'quality' means for each of the criteria introduced for successful completion of the role play, with appropriate suggestions for improvement. Of course, any Assessment for Learning (AfL) technique discussed needs practice and regular integration into language lessons for it to become really effective. Traffic lighting provides a perfect mechanism for authentic use of the target language in, for example, the instance provided by one German teacher. At appropriate junctures in the lesson, she would ask the students in German how well they had understood the focus of learning and would say *Alles klar?* She would then switch on the German-speaking traffic light construction that recites the rhyme German children learn for road safety thus:

Bei rot bleibst du stehen.
Bei grün darfst du gehen.
Bei gelb must du sehen.

The students who had learnt the rhyme would then be asked to make their own decision and to say one of the following responses:

Ich bleibe stehen.
Ich darf gehen.
Ich muss schauen.

This exercise provided an opportunity to use the target language meaningfully, to exploit a cultural and cross-curricular dimension – road safety in German schools – as well as providing key feedback to the teacher.

The traffic light technique was observed in one Scottish primary MFL classroom where each child had three teddy bears, one green, one orange and one red (real or cardboard cut-outs). The teacher would ask the children to hold up a selected bear to indicate their understanding. The children did this with self-consciousness and thus were developing self-confidence in self-assessment at Key Stage 1.

As well as reporting improved learning outcomes, many teachers have told us that one of the most significant results of engaging students in self-assessment is that they are better able to help the teacher to help them. When a students says: 'I can't do it' the teacher's usual response is 'What can't you do?' Often, the student's response is: 'I can't do any of it.' Contrast this to the comment given below by a student to the poster activity on recycling discussed above:

I know how to say 'you can' – it's 'on peut' but I'm not sure about how to tell people in the poster what they should do.

As students become more autonomous as learners, the teacher's role is recast. Instead of being both judge and jury, the teacher becomes the students' coach, mutually engaged in helping the students to reach the highest achievement they can.

9. Formative use of summative tests

Formative assessment can be useful with respect to preparation for tests. A test can provide a formative learning opportunity if it is presented as a challenge and shared, at least in part, in advance with the students to focus their learning. Students can use traffic light icons as a guide to their revision. They can create spidergrams, traffic-lighting what they know and are less sure of on an ongoing basis, thus creating a good basis for eventual revision. Teachers can analyse test results to see which items cause the main problems and then return the tests to the students, asking them to mark one another's answers to those questions, inventing the mark scheme themselves. This enables students to adopt a more detached view and reflect on what counts as a quality piece of work.

A teacher could give her class the end-of-topic test in the first lesson of the topic so that the students could use traffic-light icons to indicate their familiarity with the skills or the understanding required as part of 'advance organising', a learning strategy identified by Chamot and O'Malley (1991) as advantageous in progressing language learning. Teacher and students can then plan to focus on ways to work on the areas of unfamiliarity or difficulty. In the King's College formative assessment project (Black *et al.* 2003), some teachers who did this activity found that when the test was given at the end of the topic, the average mark for the class had risen significantly when compared with similar classes in the same year and with the teacher's same-aged class in the previous year. Clearly, the same assessment can function both summatively and formatively.

Finally, practice tests can be used formatively as part of revision. Normally, when students take practice tests, they sit the tests under examination conditions, the teacher marks the test papers, and then the teacher goes over the test with the students. While this may provide some feedback to the students, they are in very passive roles, and engagement is a problem. An alternative is to get the students to take the test under examination conditions, but then to give the test papers back to the students, unmarked, and for the students, in groups of four or five, to construct the

best *composite* response they can. Once this is done, the teacher can then hold a whole-class discussion, asking each group for their answers to each question in turn. This provides an opportunity to revise material, and to discuss examination technique.

10. Teachers learning together and putting it into practice

Developing formative practices provides an ideal focus for the development of collaborative teacher learning and for the deepening of subject knowledge. A fundamental change in practice can only be successfully implemented, as research shows, when teachers believe in what they are doing and have the time and resources to support changing practice. The best way to implement these changes is to work as a team and with a plan, that, like a work in progress, can be amended and taken forward. In order to implement the plan, the team members need time to talk to one another, run ideas past each other, share experiences, successes and disappointments, and also to observe one another's classroom work.

An audit should take place to determine what aspects of formative assessment are already being carried out so as to be able to build on these. Teachers might then review various possible improvements and changes, and decide what to try out. The whole team might try the same activity, or different members might start with different activities. AfL offers scope for teachers to take on different areas for development according to their interest and for the benefit of their colleagues. Thus one teacher could take the lead and pilot peer-assessment, while other colleagues consider target-setting and yet others take a lead on developing effective questioning techniques. Implementing these changes also means revisiting schemes of work to ensure that there are appropriate and well-spaced assessment activities in order to make the transition to more formative techniques manageable.

The teaching environment is important in an AfL approach, and teachers might create materials to support learning using posters, mobiles, charts, etc. which present key target language questions, structures and models of quality work, student-friendly mark schemes and success criteria for key tasks. It is important to change surely but slowly, starting off with just a few practices in order that the new practices can become embedded in existing valid ones.

Feedback and evaluation should be ongoing, in terms of mutual observation and of sharing of ideas, thus providing feedback and feed-forward for sustainable practices and further development. In the most effective contexts, students are involved in the developments and their feedback is valued as part of the learning community, and parents are kept well informed.

Developing a formative approach provides an excellent opportunity for collaborative MFL departmental professional development and subject leadership. This involves sharing tasks and playing to individual strengths, in itself modelling the core principles of a formative approach. AfL is about adopting certain techniques and practices but it involves primarily a new mindset and attitude. The approach provides illumination and coherence for all in the language learning project and fits well with the current culture of language learning as dialogic and interactive and with a conception of students as reflective, autonomous and strategic language learners.

References

Barnes, M. and Hunt, M. (2003) *Effective Assessment in MFL*. London: CILT.

Black, P., Harrison, C., Lee, C., Marshall, B. and Wiliam, D. (2002) *Working Inside the Black Box: Assessment for Learning in the Classroom*. London: nferNelson.

Black, P., Harrison, C., Lee, C., Marshall, B. and Wiliam, D. (2003) *Assessment for Learning: Putting it into Practice*. Maidenhead: Open University Press.

Black, P. and Wiliam, D. (1998a) 'Assessment and classroom learning.' *Assessment in Education: Principles, Policy and Practice*, 5(1), 7–73.

Black, P. and Wiliam, D. (1998b) *Inside the Black Box*. London: nferNelson.

Butler, R. (1987) 'Task-involving and ego-involving properties of evaluation: effects of different feedback conditions on motivational perceptions, interest and performance.' *Journal of Educational Psychology*, 79(4), 474–82.

Chamot, J. and O'Malley, A. (1991) *Learning Strategies in Second Language Acquisition*. Cambridge: Cambridge University Press.

Cooke, V. (2001) 'Using the first language in the classroom.' *Canadian Modern Language Review*, 57(3), 402–23.

Council of Europe (2001) *A Common European Framework for Teaching, Learning and Assessing Languages*. Cambridge: Cambridge University Press.

Crooks, T. J. (1988) 'The impact of classroom evaluation practices on students.' *Review of Educational Research*, 58(4), 438–81.

DfES (2004) *Assessment for Learning: Whole-school and Subject-specific Training Materials*. London: DfES (http://

www.standards.dfes.gov.uk/keystage3/ respub/afl_ws – accessed November 2007).

Dickens, W. T. and Flynn, J. R. (2001) 'Heritability estimates versus large environmental effects: the IQ paradox resolved.' *Psychological Review*, 108, 346–69.

Dweck, C. S. (2000) *Self-theories: Their Role in Motivation, Personality and Development*. Philadelphia, PA: Psychology Press.

Harris, R. J. and Nelson, E. M. M. (1992) 'Bilingualism: not the exception anymore,' in R. J. Harris (ed.), *Cognitive Processing in Bilinguals* (Vol. 83, pp. 3–14). Amsterdam: North Holland.

Jones, B. and Swarbrick, A. (2004) *It Makes You Think! Creating Engagement, Offering Challenges*. London: CILT.

Jones, J. (2005) 'Foreign languages in the primary school in England: a new pupil learning continuum.' *Francophonie*, 31, 3–7.

Jones, J. and Coffey, S. (2006) *Modern Foreign Languages 5–11: A Guide for Teachers*. London: David Fulton.

Lee, J., Buckland, D. and Shaw, G. (1998) *The Invisible Child*. London: CILT.

McPake, J., Johnstone, R., Low, L. and Lyall, L. (1999) *Foreign Languages in the Upper Secondary School: A Study of the Causes of Decline* (SCRE Research Report no. 91). Glasgow: University of Glasgow SCRE Centre.

Mercer, N., Dawes, L., Wegerif, R. and Sams, C. (2004) 'Reasoning as a scientist: ways of helping children to use language to learn science.' *British Educational Research Journal*, 30(3), 359–77.

Natriello, G. (1987) 'The impact of evaluation processes on students.' *Educational Psychologist*, 22(2), 155–75.

Sinclair, J. and Coulthard, M. (1975) *Towards an Analysis of Discourse*. Oxford: Oxford University Press.

Wiliam, D., Lee, C., Harrison, C. and Black, P. J. (2004) 'Teachers developing assessment for learning: impact on student achievement.' *Assessment in Education: Principles, Policy and Practice*, 11(1), 49–65.